Discovering

Washington, D. C.

Discovering

Washington, D. C.

Text: R. R. Galliher
& Barbara J. Shangle

Photo Caption Text: Barbara J. Shangle

Concept and Design: Robert D. Shangle

First Printing June, 2001
American Products Publishing Company
Division of American Products Corporation
6750 SW 111th Avenue, Beaverton, Oregon 97008

"Learn about America in a beautiful way."

Library of Congress Cataloging-in-Publication Data

Galliher, R. R., - 1940
    Discovering Washington, D. C. / text, R. R. Galliher
        p. cm.
    ISBN 1-884958-72-9 (hardcover) – ISBN 1-884958-71-0 (pbk)

    1. Washington (D. C.)—Pictorial works. 2. Washington (D. C.)—Description and travel.

    3. Washington (D. C.)—History. I. Title

F195.G35 2000
975.3—dc21   00-067515

Contents

Introduction

Washington, D. C. may be the model of national capitals. "It is the only large city in the world," wrote Washington sage Willard M. Kipplinger, "devoted exclusively to government, without the leavening of other normal human occupations." London is one of the world's largest banking centers and one of the world's greatest deep-water ports. Paris and Moscow are major centers of international trade and manufacture and lie on important navigable waterways. If any of these were suddenly to lose its governmental function, it would go right on playing a major role in the life of its nation and the world. If Washington, D. C. was to lose its governmental purpose, this city would be viewed in a much different manner.

When in 1790 Congress asked George Washington to select a site for the newly authorized federal capital "somewhere in the vicinity of the Potomac River" and "not exceeding ten-miles square," (ten miles on a side) the first President responded like the former soldier and surveyor that he was. He first did a careful and systematic reconnaissance of the land, up and down the river's edge, for some ninety miles. Then he made his recommendation. There can be little doubt that he made the best choice. In the beauty of its natural surroundings and on its admirable accessibility, the area still works well as a national capital, even two-hundred years later. Nothing could have been more appropriate than Congress naming the district for George Washington.

The original grants of land from Maryland and Virginia provided the new District of Columbia with a generous one-hundred-square-miles in which to grow. By the 1840s this seemed to be more than would ever be used and so the portion west of the river was receded to Virginia at her request. This reduced the District to its present sixty-eight-square-miles, a sloping V-shaped plain between the Potomac River on the west, a majestic one-mile-wide at this point, and the short, but broad, Anacostia River on the east.

Despite its somewhat swampy character, the site and terrain were ideally suited for the imperial capital envisioned by Pierre L'Enfant, the spirited former French military engineer appointed by George Washington to help lay out the city. The Frenchman dreamed of a super-Paris or a Constantinople, known today as Istanbul, Turkey; with boulevards 400 feet wide, of grand public monuments, vast plazas, magnificent distant views, all set off by acres and acres of lavishly cultivated greenery. Before he could give form to his dream, L'Enfant ran afoul of the country's first real estate lobby. It didn't take much figuring for the early land speculators to realize that the Frenchman's ambitious dimensions were not leaving much of that one-hundred-square-miles for their tenements. Their protest was loud and strong.

At first George Washington stood firm and backed his city planner. In time, however, he terminated the headstrong L'Enfant, just to keep peace. Happily for the nation, before the Frenchman could be ordered to roll up his steel tape, he managed to fix his indelible stamp on the face of the city. In the 1870s President Ulysses Grant directed the Commissioner of Public Works, Alexander "Box" Shepherd, to dust off L'Enfant's plan and finish the lavish job as best he could. Shepherd did an outstanding job.

Although he did not live to see it, L'Enfant's plan was realized: broad boulevards and grand vistas, elaborate monuments and public squares; and a wealth of greenery that added grandeur to the magnificent city. Early on it must have been discovered that a startling variety of trees, shrubs, and flowers would thrive in the mild, moist climate of the Potomac basin. Many exotic varieties were introduced into the city landscape, often by Americans who had served abroad, or later by members of the large international community.

It is possible that Washington, D. C. exceeds all other American cities in the amount of space reserved for growing things. Officially, there are almost 8,000 acres of land dedicated to park land, found in over 750 parks, ranging in size from giant Rock Creek with 1,754 acres, down to special playgrounds for preschool children. It is no surprise that Washington, D. C. appears as a green expanse punctuated by white buildings when viewed from the air. Add to the park lands the campus sites of twelve universities and colleges, the land of the National Arboretum, the spacious grounds of institutions such as St. Elizabeth's Hospital, the Washington Cathedral, the Franciscan Monastery, and Walter Reed Medical Center, and Washington, D. C. is a land of vivid greenery.

In reality Washington has several "faces," and it is possible to use architecture to identify different parts of the city. From the Library of Congress to the John F. Kennedy Center for the Performing Arts, and from Pennsylvania Avenue to the Potomac River, the dominant structure is the massive stone building, usually incorporating some classical, renaissance, or medieval motives. North of Pennsylvania Avenue, generally as far as Massachusetts Avenue, is considered to be "downtown," an area of white brick, concrete, steel, and glass constructed office buildings, stores, hotels, and restaurants. This is the city's central retail and financial district. Much of the remainder of the District is residential, and if it has a characteristic structure, it is the brick row houses, especially east of the Capitol and in Georgetown. Made from iron-rich local clay, the building bricks give the houses an unmistakable appearance. The larger houses — and this would be true in Georgetown, also — are sometimes classics of the Federal style. Even the small houses have a special charm and often feature bay windows, cast-iron fences around tiny yards, and brick walkways shaded by small Ailanthus trees, known commonly as the Tree of Heaven.

Like most cities, Washington has its mythology: the collection of stories longtime residents like to tell about "what it's really like" to live there. Stories of this nature tend to consist mainly of complaints, to be sure, but in order to survive, they have to be at least partly true. A quick rundown of things that are repeatedly said about Washington would have to include the summers, the winters, the traffic, the night life, and the ambience.

Complaints about the weather fall into two rather unremarkable categories: heat and humidity in summer, cold and snow in winter. A look at the record book will show that the District, in fact, does not excel in either of the measurable aspects of summer mugginess, but on a sweltering August day, it is not much consolation to know that it is even worse in Houston, Biloxi, and Terre Haute. The snow is something else again. Washington, D. C. winters are statistically mild, so that snow removal equipment has never been an item in the District's budget. However, when it gets around to snowing, it snows an abundant amount: nineteen inches in one blizzard in 1979 for instance. When this happens, activities in Washington, D. C. slip and slide to a standstill.

Washington traffic is legendary, and no story of the city is complete without some mention of the Lincoln Memorial Circle. It is true that L'Enfant's grand design did not take the automobile into account, since the city's design and the city itself are both older than the automobile. The trick, of course, is to know where you want to go and the route to use to get there, but even then the pace and aggressiveness of the drivers may come as a surprise.

Comments about the night life have one main thrust: there isn't much. This, of course, is hard to gauge: Washington appears, at least, to have enough cocktail bars, taverns, night clubs, theater and cultural events to accommodate the people who enjoy them. The District resident, in fact, may be inclined to think there is too much night life, rather than too little, but he would be taking into account the enormous volume of official entertaining that takes place behind closed doors in the foreign embassies and private homes of officials at all levels.

It has also been said of Washington, D. C. that it lacks the instantly recognizable character of a New York, San Francisco, or New Orleans. That is true, but the reason Washington, D. C. is not much like any of those places is because it is recognized as a city with a different ring to it. Anyone who has lived and worked in the capital is likely to agree that there is an unmistakable feel about the place. In some non-definable way, it is like no other city on earth. The city maintains a certain charm because of its historical significance, and perhaps it is because it has the excitement that is inescapable at the seat of the world's most powerful government. But underlying the excitement and the charm is a mysterious local atmosphere of tentativeness, a sense of impermanence. This may go far back in the city's history, to an era when a shift in administration meant, in effect, a shift in population because all jobs were political. Even today the Washingtonian is likely not to be a native of the city.

There may never have been a time since its founding that Washington has been free of talk about moving the Federal Government elsewhere. It reached a kind of crescendo after the Civil War, when it was seriously proposed in Congress that the capital be relocated in the Mississippi Valley. Throughout the 1950s the most unquenchable rumor in a rumor-ridden city was that the Government would be moved to Denver, Colorado, "to guard against atomic attack and economize on air conditioning." But now it seems there has been an unconscious decision to forget about moving elsewhere and settle in on the banks of the Potomac River forever. It is about time, too, because neither the Government nor anyone else is likely to find a prettier or more pleasant place to do business.

A School Trip
Through Washington

I n the years immediately following World War II, one of the Washington, D. C. papers could be counted on to run a late winter news story with a headline reading: "Capital Braces. Estimate Two-Million Visitors." Maybe the figure was only one million; but whatever it was, at the time it seemed like a great many. Today, the capital handles more than twenty-million-plus visitors a year, and the figure keeps rising. Buried among these millions is that loyal core of springtime school excursionists, college students, and American families — the bulk of the visitors — and an increasing number of foreign visitors. It is a good bet that virtually the entire twenty-million-plus visitors return home even more enthusiastic about the nation's capital than when they arrived. The reason is obvious. Washington, D. C. is just about the most enjoyable destination in the history of travel.

For anyone who is intellectually curious, the capital city can be endlessly fascinating. In the 2.5 miles separating the Folger Shakespeare Library on Capitol Hill from the Kennedy Center for the Performing Arts, overlooking the Potomac River, there may be more engrossing sights and activities than in any comparable stretch in the world. Even if the curious visitor didn't read a single book from the mountainous volumes at the Library of Congress, his lifetime might be consumed trying to have a look at the millions and millions of items in the custody of the Smithsonian Institution. An unbridled amount of time is required to view the National Gallery of Art, or to rummage through the millions of records in the National Archives. Fatigue or old age could set in long before the visitor reached the top of the Washington Monument, toured the White House, saw the population "clock" at the Department of Commerce building, and heard a concert at the Kennedy Center.

The best advice to a visitor is to stroll around a bit and see the city from the outside of the buildings before plunging into its museums, galleries, and public buildings. In fact, a walk down The National Mall, a green grass expanse extending from the United States Capitol to the Washington Monument, a distance of about two miles, is probably a good prescription for cooling the senses and getting accustomed to the scale of the place. The broad marble steps of John Russell Pope's National Gallery of Art, or the edge of the Reflecting Pool that leads from the Washington Monument to the steps of the Lincoln Memorial, invites resting and contemplation. A return route up the south side of The Mall will take the stroller past its oldest completed structure, the red sandstone "Castle" of the Smithsonian Institution. Back on Capitol Hill—referred to simply as "the Hill" in Washington talk—the visitor is sure to have a deepened appreciation of L'Enfant's "noble prospect" as he looks westward over The Mall toward the Virginia hills.

Before the *air* age, most visitors were introduced to the nation's capital as they stepped from the darkness of the lovable cavernous old Union Station into the Plaza. Few thrills can match that first sudden sight of the great white dome of the Capitol looming above the trees, the noise of the cars and taxis around the Columbus Monument Circle. The visitor finds himself at the hub of the nation's business. A few minutes walk would see him shaking hands with one of his two Senators at one of three buildings provided for Senate use: the

Philip A. Hart Senate Office Building, the Richard B. Russell Senate Office Buildling, or the Everett M. Dirksen Senate Office Building. After another short walk, he could be standing in the Capitol rotunda.

The Union Station was completed in 1908 by the Pennsylvania and the Ohio & Baltimore railroads, bringing pride to the city as well as an expansive transportation system, enabling easier access to the nation's working center of government. Dignitaries of the United States and foreign countries were greeted with style and departed with fanfare from this magnificent building. As air service pushed train travel back during the late 1950s and '60s as a primary way to travel across this nation, the importance of Union Station reflected the standard activity in most train stations across the nation, dwindling to little activity and eventual closure. Efforts were made to create usage of the Station during the late 1960s and '70s, but little came of it, except money being spent to renew the onetime glamour of the old building. A renewed effort burst forth in the early 1980s, renovating the structure to a grandness equal to its original style. Today, the trains power in and out of the terminal; millions of people stroll through the historical hallways visiting any one of the over 130 sales shops and restaurants that echo exuberant activity, bringing life back to one of the more popular buildings in Washington, D. C. Union Station states that it "is the most exciting and dynamic shopping destination in the country. The quality and diversity of its stores have made it the choice of Presidents as well as millions of busy commuters and wide-eyed tourists each year."

In Washington, D. C. all things seem to relate to the Capitol, even the streets radiate from it, dividing the city into quadrants. The original design for the Capitol came from an amateur architect, William Thornton, a Scottish physician who won a contest. In 1792 then Secretary of State Thomas Jefferson suggested a contest that would reward the winning design a "$500 prize and a city lot." The building was constructed in fits and starts, definitely hampered by its burning in 1814 by the British during the War of 1812. It really wasn't finished until 1863 when the massive cast-iron dome designed by Thomas Ustick Walter was raised over the original dome atop the marble structure. Additions have been made to the capitol, however, such as between 1884 and 1891 when grand marble terraces were added to the West Front. Completed in 1960, the East Front experienced structural changes with an expansion of 32.5 feet that added 102 rooms to the marble building. Inside the Capitol there is much for the visitor to see—the profound Rotunda, the Old House and Senate chambers, committee meeting rooms, statuary, murals, inscriptions, interesting architecture and acoustics, and the Senate Subway.

The visitor may welcome the brisk walk across the East Capitol Plaza to reach the severely classical, white marble front of the United States Supreme Court Building. The Supreme Court has occupied part of the Capitol through most of its history, and when it was housed in its own building in the 1930s, it seemed natural that it would be on the Hill. Inside the massive structure, architect Cass Gilbert's building is rich in marble, heavy wood paneling, thick carpeting, and velour trappings. The solemn, muffled atmosphere makes plain that some weighty thinking goes on behind those heavy doors. The great spiral staircase is a surprise feature and its elliptical curves help soften somewhat the building's angular severity.

Immediately south of the Supreme Court building is the green-domed building housing the Library of Congress, a Renaissance architectural designed structure named the Jefferson Building in honor of Thomas Jefferson. In contrast the studied absence of decoration from the attractive Annex—The Adams Building, named for John Adams— helps to strike a startling balance between the two as they face each other across Second Street Southeast. The Library of Congress owns the world's largest library and has custody to about 119-million items spread upon some 530 miles of bookshelves located in several locations.

The United States Capitol

"The United States Capitol is among the most architecturally impressive and symbolically important buildings in the world. It has housed the meeting chambers of the Senate and the House of Representatives for almost two centuries. Begun in 1793, the Capitol has been built, burnt, rebuilt, extended, and restored: today, it stands as a monument not only to its builders but also to the American people and their government." (*www.aoc.gov*) Grand marble terraces grace the west front of the Capitol, which were added to the building between 1884 and 1891. Continued restoration work has allowed the beauty of the building to be maintained at its grand design.

Photography by Shangle Photographics

The White House

"For two hundred years, the White House has stood as a symbol of the Presidency, the United States government, and the American people. Its history, and the history of the nation's capital, began when President George Washington signed an Act of Congress in December of 1790 declaring that the federal government would reside in a district 'not exceeding ten miles square...on the river Potomac.' President Washington, together with city planner Pierre L'Enfant, chose the site for the new residence, which is now 1600 Pennsylvania Avenue. As preparations began for the new federal city, a competition was held to find a builder of the 'President's House.' Nine proposals were submitted, and Irish-born architect James Hoban won a gold medal for his practical and handsome design.... Construction began when the first cornerstone was laid in October 1792. Although President Washington oversaw the construction of the house, he never lived in it. It was not until 1800, when the White House was nearly completed that its first resident, President John Adams and his wife, Abigail, moved in... [The White House is] the only private residence of a head of state that is open to the public, free of charge." (*www.whitehouse.gov*)
Photography by Shangle Photographics

The Washington Monument

The Washington Monument Society, founded by John Marshall and James Madison in 1833, took up the cause to honor the outstanding patriot, George Washington, often referred to as the "Father of our Country." Many obstacles along the way slowed the completion of the monument, often to a stand still during the Civil War. The monument was finally dedicated February 21, 1885, and opened for public tours October 9, 1888. The building reaches 555 feet, 5 1/8th inches into the sky, with a thrusting "unadorned Egyptian obelisk" made of Maryland and Massachusetts marble, much granite and interior ironwork. A recent extensive restoration program has brought the building to a modern marvel, aided by private and corporate funds from patriot supporters.

Photography by James Blank

The United States Supreme Court Building

Words of value grace both the west entrance, with *Equal Justice Under the Law,* and the east entrance, with *Justice the Guardian of Liberty.* That style of guidance has persevered since the first session of the court that took place on February 1, 1790, in New York City in the Royal Exchange Building. The Court has had many homes before settling into the new house in 1935. Philadelphia, Pennsylvania, provided chambers in Independence Hall and the City Hall from 1790 to 1800, at which time the Court moved to the new capital, Washington, D. C. When the nation's Capitol was burned by the British in the War of 1812, the Court convened in a private residence. When the Capitol was restored for occupancy, the Supreme Court was lodged in what is referred to as the "Old Supreme Court Chamber" from 1816 to 1860, moving to the "Old Senate Chamber," where the Court maintained presence until this handsome marble structure was built. Sixteen marble columns support the heavily adorned portico and 100-foot wide oval plaza, delivering a strong character to a supreme building that is home to nine justices.

Photography by James Blank

The Bureau of Engraving and Printing

"The establishment of the Bureau of Engraving and Printing can be traced as far back as August 29, 1862, to a single room in the basement of the main Treasury building where two men and four women separated and sealed by hand $1 and $2 United States Notes which had been printed by private bank note companies. Today there are approximately 2,500 employees who work out of two buildings in Washington, D. C. and a new facility located in Fort Worth, Texas." (*www.moneyfactor.com*) The Bureau of Engraving and Printing state that the Bureau produces about 120-billion-dollars a year, printed on large sheets. The individual bills are cut to size by an ordinary paper cutting machine, as used in a typical printing business. All of the U. S. postage stamps are printed by the Bureau of Engraving and Printing. One interesting responsibility of the Secretary of the Treasury includes the selection of designs and portraits that appear on the U. S. currency. The Great Seal of the United States first appeared on the one-dollar Federal Reserve note in 1935.
Photography by James Blank

The Thomas Jefferson Memorial and the Tidal Basin

"The Thomas Jefferson Memorial, modeled after the Pantheon of Rome, is America's foremost memorial to our third president. As an original adaptation of Neoclassical architecture, it is a key landmark in the monumental core of Washington, D. C. The circular, colonnaded structure in the classic style was introduced to this country by Thomas Jefferson. Architect John Russell Pope used Jefferson's own architectural tastes in the design of the Memorial. His intention was to synthesize Jefferson's contribution as a statesman, architect, President, drafter of the Declaration of Independence, advisor of the Constitution and founder of the University of Virginia.... The present-day location at the Tidal Basin was selected in 1937.... On November 15, 1939, a ceremony was held in which President Roosevelt laid the cornerstone of the Memorial." *(National Park Service)* The Memorial was officially dedicated on December 19, 1943, commemorating the 200th anniversary of Jefferson's birth. A nineteen-foot bronze statue of Thomas Jefferson, set upon a six-foot high, black-granite pedestal, graces the center of the rotunda, gazing out across the Tidal Basin toward the nation's capitol. "Each year the Jefferson Memorial plays host to various ceremonies, including annual Memorial exercises, Easter Sunrise Services and the ever-popular Cherry Blossom Festival. The Jefferson Memorial is administered and maintained by the National Park Service. " (*National Park Service*)

Photography by James Blank

22

The National Museum of American History

The National Museum of American History is part of the complex Smithsonian Institution and opened its doors to the public in January, 1964, as the Museum of History and Technology. In October, 1980, the name was changed "to better represent its basic mission—the collection, care, and study of objects that reflect the experience of the American people.... The Museum's area is approximately 750,000 square feet, including a basement, three main exhibition levels, two office-collection levels, and a mechanical penthouse on the roof. The space includes workshops, laboratories, offices, libraries, archives, and other support areas along with an auditorium, a bookstore, gift shops, public and staff cafeterias, an ice cream parlor, and a working post office. "(*National Museum of American History*) Extensive hands-on-tours are available for the taking.
Photography by James Blank

The United States Marine Corps War Memorial

"The Marine Corps War Memorial stands as a symbol of this grateful Nation's esteem for the honored dead of the U. S. Marine Corps. While the statue depicts one of the most famous incidents of World War II, the memorial is dedicated to all Marines who have given their lives in the defense of the United States since 1775.... Burnished in gold on the granite [base] are the names and dates of every principal Marine Corps engagement since the founding of the Corps, as well as the inscription: 'In honor and in memory of the men of the United States Marine Corps who have given their lives to their country since November 10, 1775.' Also inscribed on the base is the tribute of Fleet Adm. Chester W. Nimitz to the fighting men on Iwo Jima: 'Uncommon Valor was a Common Virtue.' " (*www.nps.gov*) The flag flies twenty-four hours a day at the end of a sixty-foot bronze pole.

Photography by James Blank

The United States Department of the Treasury

The National Park Service states that the "present Treasury Building was built over a period of 33 years between 1836 and 1869. [It] is the oldest department building in Washington and has had a great impact on the design of other governmental buildings. At the time of its completion, it was one of the largest office buildings in the world. It served as a barracks for soldiers during the Civil War and as the temporary White House for President Andrew Johnson following the assassination of President Lincoln in 1865." "The stone used in the South Wing, the West Wing and the North Wing was quarried on Dix Island, near Rockland, Maine, and transported in sailing vessels. The facades are adorned by monolithic columns of the Ionic order, each 36 feet tall and weighing 30 tons. Each column cost $5,000. There are 34 of these pillars on the east side of the building facing Fifteenth Street, 30 of them forming a colonnade 341 feet long.... There are 18 column[s] on the west side and ten each on the north and south sides.... The Main Treasury Building covers five stories and a raised basement and sits on 5 acres of ground. The building measures 466 feet north to south by 260 feet east to west." (*www.treas.gov*)
Photography by James Blank

25

The Lincoln Memorial

"The Lincoln Memorial stands at the west end of the National Mall as a neoclassical monument to the 16th President. The memorial, designed by Henry Bacon, after ancient Greek temples, stands 190 feet long, 119 feet wide, and almost 100 feet high. It is surrounded by a peristyle of 36 fluted Doric columns, one for each of the thirty six states in the Union at the time of Lincoln's death, and two columns [sic] in-antis at the entrance behind the colonnade.... Lying between the north and south chambers is the central hall containing the solitary figure of Lincoln sitting in contemplation.... Construction began in 1914, and the memorial was opened to the public in 1922." (*www.nps.gov*) The Memorial is not only a tribute to Abraham Lincoln but it is also a symbol of American Democracy and the freedom that has been maintained through the unity of the people of this nation.

Photography by James Blank

The Vietnam Veterans Memorial

"The Vietnam Veterans Memorial Wall contains the names of the 58,220 men and women who were killed and remain missing from that war. The names are etched on black granite panels that compose the Wall. The panels are arranged into two arms, extending from a central point to form a wide angle. Each arm points to either the Washington Monument [as shown in the background] or the Lincoln Memorial...bring the Vietnam Memorial into an historical context on the National Mall. The Wall is built into the earth, below ground level. The area within the Wall's angle has been contoured to form a gentle sloped approach towards the center of the Wall...a place of quiet, calmness, and serenity." *(National Park Service)*
Photography by James Blank

The statue of Thomas Jefferson at the Thomas Jefferson Memorial

Thomas Jefferson: author of the Declaration of Independence, third president of the United States, and founder of the University of Virginia, which he considered his finest achievement in life. He was born April 13, 1743, and died July 4, 1826.

Photography by Shangle Photographics

Korean War Veterans Memorial

"General Douglas MacArthur said, 'Old soldiers never die, they just fade away.' When the last of the Korean War veterans fades into history he can do so knowing that a portion of the National Mall in Washington, D. C. has been set aside to remind future generations of what they did for Freedom. Those veterans that are still with us today can be assured that they are forgotten no more. The many parts of the Korean War Veterans Memorial should be viewed as a whole and not separately. The statues depicting fighting men on patrol represent all four branches of the United States military working together for a common goal...victory. These men would fight alongside the men of many other nations. These nations are listed on the United Nations Wall, bordering one side of the statues. The opposite wall is lined with etchings of the faces of the men and women who supported the United States' effort on the front lines. All of these various elements point towards the Pool of Remembrance, an area where the sacrifice of 54,269 American lives can be contemplated and remembered. It is here where an inscription summarizes the true meaning of the memorial: *Our nation honors her sons and daughters who answered the call to defend a country they never knew and a people they never met.*" (*www.nps.gov*)
Photography by Marian Blank

Tomb of the Unknowns at Arlington National Cemetery, Arlington, Virginia

"The Tomb of the Unknowns, near the center of the cemetery, is one of Arlington's most popular tourist sites. The Tomb contains the remains of unknown American soldiers from World Wars I and II, the Korean Conflict and (until 1998) the Vietnam War. Each was presented with the Medal of Honor at the time of interment and the medals, as well as the flags which covered their caskets, are on display inside the Memorial Amphitheater, directly to the rear of the Tomb. The Tomb is guarded 24-hours-per-day and 365-days-per year by specially trained members of the 3rd United States Infantry (The Old Guard)." *(www.arlingtoncemetery.com)* The white Colorado-marble sarcophagus resides over the grave of the World War I unknown soldier; to the west are the marble crypts of the Unknown Soldiers of World War II, the Korean Conflict, and the crypt honoring the Vietnam Unknown, which now remains vacant since the Unknown, laid to rest in 1984, was tentatively identified and exhumed in 1998.

Photography by James Blank

The Washington Monument and the Lincoln Memorial Reflecting Pool

The tree-lined Reflecting Pool, situated between the Washington Monument and the Lincoln Memorial in western Washington, D. C., lives up to its name. The Constitution Gardens edge both sides of the pool for over one-third mile.
Photography by James Blank

Arlington National Cemetery, Arlington, Virginia

As far as the eye can see, rows of markers that meet the requirements established for the national cemetery exhaust themselves across the cemetery grounds: "These monuments will be of simple design, dignified, and appropriate to a military cemetery." The cemetery is divided into sections that are designated for particular groups: Astronauts, Civilians, Foreign Nationals, Medal of Honor recipients, U. S. Air Force, U. S. Army, U. S. Coast Guard, U. S. Marines, and the U. S. Navy. "Tucked away on the other side of the cemetery, in Section 27, near the Netherlands Carillon and the Marine Corps Memorial, stand more than 3,800 grave markers with inscriptions bearing the words 'civilian' and 'citizen.' The people buried there were once residents of Freedman's Village during and after the Civil War.... There are 2,111 Civil War Unknowns buried together in section 26." (*www.arlingtoncemetery.com*) There are over 280,000 people buried at Arlington National Cemetery.

Photography by James Blank

Tomb of the Unknowns, Arlington National Cemetery, Arlington, Virginia

Often referred to as the Tomb of the Unknown Soldier, the Tomb of the Unknowns has never officially been named, according to information released by the Military District of Washington. Approval for the Monument took place March 4, 1921. The selection of an Unknown Soldier to rest in the Tomb is performed by an individual who, by his own merit, has displayed distinguished service and valor, having received such honors as the Distinguished Service Medal and the Medal of Honor, during each of the time-periods honored. More than one body is received for selection, each casket appearing the same, without identification. A simple rose placed upon one of the caskets at the time of arbitrary selection is enough to place the honor onto an Unknown Soldier. Supreme respect is bestowed on the other chosen soldiers for possible inclusion, but not selected for special interment. Presidents Warren Harding, Dwight D. Eisenhower, and Ronald Reagan were active participants during the interments that occurred during their administrations.
Photography by James Blank

Union Station

The whistle of a train has meant much to Washington, D. C. over the years. Completed in 1908 by the Pennsylvania and the Ohio & Baltimore Railroads, the Union Station brought pride to the city as well as an expansive transportation system, enabling easier access to the nation's working center of government. Dignitaries of the United States and foreign countries were greeted with style and departed with fanfare from this magnificent building. As air service pushed train travel back during the late 1950s and '60s as a primary way to travel across this nation, the importance of Union Station reflected the standard activity in most train stations across the nation, dwindling to little activity and eventual closure. Efforts were made to create usage of the Station during the late 1960s and '70s, but little came of it, except money being spent to renew the onetime glamour of the old building. A renewed effort burst forth in the early 1980s, renovating the structure to a grandness equal to its original style. Today, the trains power in and out of the terminal; millions of people stroll through the historical hallways visiting any one of the over-130 sales shops and restaurants that echo exuberant activity, bringing life back to one of the more popular buildings in Washington, D. C. Union Station states that it "is the most exciting and dynamic shopping destination in the country. The quality and diversity of its stores have made it the choice of Presidents as well as millions of busy commuters and wide-eyed tourists each year."

Photography by Shangle Photographics

Howard University

Howard University honored its founder, Oliver Otis Howard, by bestowing his name onto the school founded in 1867. The initial plan in 1866 was to establish a theological seminary for the education of African-American clergymen. "The University charter, as enacted by Congress and subsequently approved by President Andrew Johnson on March 2, 1867, designated Howard University as 'a university for the education of youth in the liberal arts and sciences.' " Through its Vision Statement the University goes on to say that "Howard University is a comprehensive research university, unique and irreplaceable, defined by its core values, the excellence of all its activities—its instruction, research and service—and by its enduring commitment to educating youth, African Americans and other people of color in particular, for leadership and service to our nation and the global community."

Photography by Shangle Photographics

35

The Washington National Cathedral

Washington, D. C. has on occasion been described as a city of churches. Since there are about five-hundred churches, this must refer to their architectural splendor. Washington National Cathedral, the biggest of the churches in the District, dominates the northwest skyline of the city, partly because of its size, and partly because it is on one of the highest spots in the city. The Cathedral is stated to be the sixth largest cathedral in the world and the second largest in the United States. Records indicate that President Theodore Roosevelt was present when the Cathedral's cornerstone was laid in 1907, and President George Herbert Walker Bush spoke when the final stone was set on September 19, 1990.
Photography by James Blank

The Memorial Amphitheater at Arlington National Cemetery, Arlington, Virginia

"The Memorial Amphitheater...was dedicated on May 15, 1920. While many ceremonies are conducted throughout the country, many consider the services at Arlington's Memorial Amphitheater to be the nation's official ceremonies to honor all American service members who serve to keep the United States free.... [There are] three major annual memorial services in the Amphitheater. They take place Easter, Memorial Day and Veterans Day and are sponsored by the U. S. Army Military District of Washington.... The Amphitheater is constructed mainly of Vermont-quarried Danby marble. The marble in the Memorial Display Room is imported Botticino, a stone mined in Italy. The Memorial Display Room, between the amphitheater and the Tomb of the Unknowns, houses plaques and other tributes presented in honor of the four service members interred at the Tomb of the Unknowns (first known as the Tomb of the Unknown Soldier). A small chapel is beneath the Amphitheater stage." (*www.arlingtoncemetery.org*)
Photography by Shangle Photographics

The Sam Rayburn House Office Building

This building is the third of three office buildings designated for use by members of the United States House of Representatives. The building is described as "a modified H plan with four stories above ground, two basements, and three levels of underground garage space. A white marble facade above a pink granite base covers a concrete and steel frame. One hundred sixty-nine Representatives were accommodated in three-room suites…. A subway tunnel with two cars connects the building to the Capitol…" (*www.aoc.gov*) A man from Texas was honored by having his name applied to this building. He was a man who served his country well, maintaining a position no other Congressional Representative has yet to exceed. Samuel Taliaferro Rayburn served the U. S. House of Representative from Texas 4th District from 1913 to 1961, serving as Speaker of the House during ten individual sessions of Congress: the 76th, 77th, 78th, 79th, 81st, 82nd, 84th, 85th, 86th, 87th, each for a period of two years. Rayburn served as House Majority Leader during the 75th and 76th Congress, and served as Minority Leader during the 80th and 83rd Congress. He was indeed a leader of men. He was born in Kingston, Tennessee, January 6, 1882, moving to Fannin County, Texas, in 1887. He graduated from East Texas Normal College in 1903; graduated from the University of Texas at Austin where he studied law; he was admitted to the bar in 1908. Sam Rayburn died in Bonham, Texas, on November 16, 1961, and was buried in Willow Wild Cemetery in Bonham.

Photography by James Blank

The grave site of President John Fitzgerald Kennedy, Arlington National Cemetery, Virginia

The 35th President of the United States was laid to rest November 25, 1963, in Arlington National Cemetery, following his assasination in Dallas, Texas, on November 22, 1963. A new site was created in March 1967, relocating the casket of the late President and his two deceased children, who had been placed beside him in December, 1963. The site was selected by his wife, Jacqueline Bouvier Kennedy; Jacqueline died in May, 1994, and was buried next to her husband. John Fitzgeral Kennedy was born in Brookline, Massachusetts, on May 29, 1917. His education centers included Harvard University and Stanford Business School, completing his formal education in 1941. He served his country in the U. S. Navy from 1941 to 1945. He began his political career as the U. S. Congressional Representative from Massachusetts serving from 1947 through 1953, when he won election to the U. S. Senate, serving until 1961. He became the 35th United States President in January, 1961. The Eternal Flame burning at the gravesite was lighted by Jacqueline Kennedy.
Photography by James Blank

Smithsonian National Air and Space Museum

The Museum states that it "maintains the largest collection of historic air and spacecraft in the world. It is also a vital center for research into the history, science, and technology of aviation and space flight."
Photo by Shangle Photographics

The Hubert H. Humphrey Building, The Department of Health and Human Services

The Department states that it "is the United States government's principal agency for protecting the health of all Americans and providing essential human services, especially for those who are least able to help themselves. The Department includes more than 300 programs…." It is designed to facilitate service for family care, support programs, preventative care, Medicare administration, and care for American and Alaska Natives. There are eleven operating divisions within the Department. History indicates that the Marine Hospital established in 1798 was the forerunner of today's Public Health Service. During Lincoln's administration in 1862 the Department of Chemistry was created, hence the Food and Drug Administration. From a one-room laboratory on Staten Island in 1887 grew the National Institutes of Health. The Social Security Act was passed by Congress in 1935. In 1939 the Federal Security Agency took shape, consolidating the fields of health, education, social insurance and human services. The Communicable Disease Center was established in 1946. The Department of Human Services was established on May 4, 1980, and activities continue.
Photography by Shangle Photographics

The United States Capitol, East Front

It was the results of a competition for the best design that brought about America's most recognized structure. A Scottish physician, Dr. William Thornton, won the "$500 prize and a city lot" as a reward for his efforts, heeding the call suggested by then Secretary of State Thomas Jefferson in 1792. The East Front experienced structural changes that were completed in 1960 with an expansion of 32.5 feet, which added 102 rooms to the marble building.

Photography by James Blank

The John F. Kennedy Center for the Performing Arts

"The Kennedy Center, located on 17 acres overlooking the Potomac River in Washington, is America's living memorial to President Kennedy as well as the nation's busiest arts facility, presenting more than 3,300 performances each year for audiences numbering more than 2 million. More than 3 million people tour the Center each year, and an additional 20 million each year attend touring Kennedy Center productions or tune in to television, radio, and Internet broadcasts. As part of the Kennedy Center's Performing Arts for Everyone outreach program, hundreds of free performances are offered each year featuring national and local artists; these include early-evening concerts on the Millennium Stage, dozens of performances during the annual Open House Arts Festival, and daily concerts of seasonal music in December as part of the Holidays at the Kennedy Center. Since 1999, each night's Millennium Stage performance has been broadcast live over the Internet, and digitally archived on the Kennedy Center's Web site." (*www.kennedy-center.org*)
Photography by Shangle Photographics

The Netherlands Carillon

As a gift from the Netherlands, the Carillon was presented to the people of the United States from the Dutch people as an expression of gratitude for the "aid received during and after World War II." The 49-bell carillon was officially dedicated on May 5, 1960, fifteen years after the liberation of the Netherlands from the German Nazis. By continued Dutch appreciation, a 50th bell was added to the Carillon on May 5, 1995, on the 50th anniversary of the liberation. The carillon tower is located on the northern end of Arlington National Cemetery near The United States Marine Corps War Memorial.
Photography by James Blank

The Mormon Temple

For many of the visitors to Washington D.C., their visit would not be complete without viewing the white marbled Washington Temple and Visitor Center. Prior to the Temple dedication in 1974, a reported 758,000 people visited the beautiful structure. "The mission of the Visitors Center is to share the precious message of the gospel of Jesus Christ with the world. The spirit found there testifies that we are all children of a loving Heavenly Father whose greatest desire is for us to find joy in this life and qualify to return to live with Him throughout eternity." (*washingtonlds.org/dctemple)* The Mormon Temple grounds are spread over 57 acres of beautifully landscaped grounds bedecked with floral gardens. The Visitor Center welcomes all people, while the Temple is only open to members of the church.

The Franklin Delano Roosevelt Memorial

The National Park Service describes the Memorial as follows: "The Franklin Delano Roosevelt Memorial is one of the most expansive memorials in the nation. Yet, its shade trees, waterfalls, statuary, and quiet alcoves create the feeling of a secluded garden rather than an imposing structure. The memorial is divided into four outdoor galleries, or rooms, one for each of FDR's terms in office. The rooms are defined by walls of red South Dakota granite and by ornamental plantings; quotations from FDR are carved into the granite. Water cascades and quiet pools are present throughout. Each room conveys in its own way the spirit of this great man." The Memorial is located along the Tidal Basin and the Cherry Tree Walk near the National Mall.

Photography by James Blank

A view of the Nation's Capitol from the Washington Monument

Elizabeth (Betsy) Ross is recognized as the original seamstress of the first national flag, referred to by members of her family as the Star Spangled Banner. She was secretly commissioned by the Continental Congress in May, 1776, to sew the first flag, which she completed in June. The following year "on June 14, 1777, the Continental Congress, seeking to promote national pride and unity, adopted the national flag. 'Resolved: that the flag of the United States be thirteen stripes, alternate red and white; that the union be thirteen stars, white in a blue field, representing a new constellation.' "

Photography by Shangle Photographics

The Lincoln Memorial

This Memorial honors the 16th President of the United States. Abraham Lincoln was born as a Sunday's child, on February 12, 1809, to Thomas and Nancy Hanks Lincoln in Hodgenville, Kentucky. Abraham was named for Thomas Lincoln's father. His mother died when he was 9-years old, while living in southern Indiana. Lincoln's life was one of austerity, but one of honor, achieving self discipline at an early age that allowed him to persevere throughout his lifetime. His life's experiences brought living achievements that catapulted him to national attention and to the Presidency of the United States in 1860. Lincoln led and served his country during the nation's most critical days of development, during the Civil War. He is remembered for many grand achievements, especially his profound written words that created the Gettysburg Address and the Emancipation Proclamation. His life was ended abruptly on April 14, 1865, Good Friday, by an assassin's bullet, fired by John Wilkes Booth.

Photography by Shangle Photographics

Ford's Theatre

This nineteenth-century style theater-playhouse reverberates today with laughter, tears of joy, and melodrama circumstances brought about by theater productions of contemporary and period drama. However, on the historical evening of April 14, 1865, the happiness and joy created by the production of *Our American Cousin* was instantly removed, and in its place a hush, and an atmosphere of great somber covered the surroundings. President Abraham Lincoln, who was attending the performance with his wife, Mary, was shot and gravely wounded by John Wilkes Booth, a onetime theatrical performer who wanted to create havoc for the Union forces, believing the death of the President would give strength to the Confederacy. President Lincoln died the next morning, April 15th. It is presumed that Booth died twelve days later during a standoff against Union soldiers where he was hiding in a barn that was set afire. There is some belief that he was successful in fleeing the scene. Ford's Theatre, a National Historic Site, is popular as a museum as well as a fine house of theater productions.

Photography by James Blank

A westward view from the Washington Monument to the Lincoln Memorial

Through a portion of a circle of United States flags that surround the Washington Monument, the tree-lined Reflecting Pool leads to the Lincoln Memorial, adding expansive space between the two structures. The city of Arlington, Virginia, looms in the background. Memorable events have taken place in this space, one being the "I Have a Dream" speech presented by Martin Luther King, Jr. on August 28, 1963, on the steps of the Lincoln Memorial. Committed to serve and to inspire others to fulfill their personal dreams and potential, Martin Luther King, Jr. is honored annually by the nation on the third Monday in January, commemorating his birthday of January 15, 1929.

Photography by James Blank

Healy Hall at Georgetown University

It was 1789 when Reverend John Carroll obtained ownership to sixty acres of ground that overlooked the settlement of Georgetown. Georgetown College was soon opened, in January, 1792, and at the end of the first academic year the enrollment reached 66 students. "The first buildings were constructed around the 'old quadrangle,' including Healy Hall," completed in 1875. Healy Hall was named for Reverend Patrick S. Healy, S.J., President of the University between 1873 to 1882. Healy Hall, a Flemish Renaissance architectural style, is on the National Register of Historic Places.
Photography by James Blank

The Three Servicemen Statue

Added to the black walled Vietnam Veterans Memorial in 1984, the statue of three typical United States soldiers, representing any one of the military branches present in Vietnam—Army, Navy, Airforce, or Marines—depicts the haunting wonder of the investigating soldier. Some say the soldiers represent the troops on patrol, while others say they are searching for their own names on the Monument wall. Sculptor Frederick Hart designed and created the statue.

Photography by Shangle Photographics

Mount Vernon

"A man's home is his castle." That is how George Washington felt about his home, located along the Potomac River south of Washington, D.C. As the commander of the Continental Army during the Revolutionary War, George spent little time at his favorite site; but following the end of the war, he and his wife, Martha, devoted their precious time to their home. Even during his eight years as the nation's first President, George Washington spent as much time as possible at his farm. George Washington was born in Westmoreland County, Virginia, on February 22, 1731. His great-grandfather received the land as a grant from King Charles II in 1674; the house seen today was built in 1735. George inherited the house and about 2,000 acres in 1761, though he lived there as a young child and again as an young man. The house and land remained in the Washington family until 1858. The Mount Vernon Ladies' Association, founded in 1853, purchased 200 acres and the Washington house from Washington's great-grandnephew. Through the efforts of the Association, the grounds, which at one time reached some 8,000 acres, the house, and supporting outbuildings have been restored to an authentic appearance and grand presentation. The estate and gardens have been reduced to a 40 acre area today, which includes the Tomb of George and Martha Washington. Washington died at Mount Vernon on December 14, 1799, at the age of 68 years. Tours are available through the house, outbuildings, and over the grounds where personal artifacts that belonged to Washington and his family are displayed, along with period furnishings.

Photography by James Blank

The Basilica of the National Shrine of the Immaculate Conception

Ground breaking for the National Shrine occurred in 1920. Through the efforts of Bishop Thomas Shahan, the fourth president of Catholic University, which is adjacent to the church, three acres of ground that belonged to the University were obtained for the expressed purpose of constructing a shrine to honor the Holy Mother, Mary. The National Shrine states that the "Basilica of the National Shrine is the largest Catholic church in the Western Hemisphere and the eighth largest in the world. It measures a total of 459 feet long and covers an area of 77,500 square feet. The Knights' Tower, a gift of the Knights of Columbus and completed in 1959, rises 329 feet from ground level. The interior of the Great Upper Church is 399 feet long and can accommodate more than six thousand worshipers. The Crypt Church is 200 feet long, 160 feet wide and can comfortably seat more than 400 persons." The National Council of Catholic Women gifted the prayer garden, Mary's Garden, in June, 2000, providing a location for personal reflection and prayer.
Photography by James Blank

The Vietnam Women's Memorial

It was November 11, 1993, when the dedication of the Vietnam Women's Memorial occurred, adding a vital and much needed tribute to the women who served during the Vietnam War, and to the families who anguished because of the war. Located near the Vietnam Memorial Wall and to the statue of the Three Servicemen, this bronze statue reflects the agony, pain, love, valor, and protection provided by the dedicated women who volunteered to serve their country and fellow man during a time of danger and hardship in Vietnam. It is reported that some 11,000 United States military women served during the war, 90% of them were nurses. On a world wide basis, the census was approximately 265,000 women serving in countries that received the wounded of the war. "The women's war was different from the men's—instead of exploding in the jungle, it blew up in the mind. Surrounded by death, the nurses had to shut down emotionally. They could not show their feelings to the soldiers they were trying to heal. Like the Vietnam Wall, the Vietnam Womens Memorial has brought healing." (*www.nps.gov/vive/memorial/women*)
Photography by Marian Blank

The National Archives

America's historical documents are housed in the National Archives, first occupied in November, 1935. The original manuscripts of the Declaration of Independence, the United States Constitution, and the Bill of Rights are but a few of the national treasures garnered for safekeeping in this building and on display for public viewing. The National Archives states that it "houses textual and microfilm records relating to genealogy, American Indians, pre-World War II military and naval-maritime matters, the New Deal, the District of Columbia, the Federal courts, and Congress."
Photography by James Blank

The Watergate

Designed for comfort, pleasure, and convenience, the Watergate complex provides all these things, and it also provides a colorful history few apartment buildings are able to provide. This building has been home to dignitaries of the United States government, to prestigious business people, and influential folks who know their way around the Washington, D.C. circles. United State Presidents have experienced grief by having connections to this building, stirring up federal investigations that have marred their historical legacy. The name, Watergate, is able to conjure up much scandal, but so can the words Crédit Mobilier, Whiskey Ring, Teapot Dome, and Iran-Contra. History is full of scandal, sad to say. All of the aforementioned are scandals going back to the 1860s. Scandal investigation has produced governmental intervention in an effort to remove the opportunity to create problems in the future. The Watergate Building has continued to provide the amenities so garnered by those who occupy the building and for those who wish and hope to occupy the building. Located along the Potomac River in Washington, D.C. proper, if you live there, you are close to work.
Photography by James Blank

The Smithsonian Institution

The Smithsonian Institution states it best: "The Smithsonian Institution was established in 1846 with funds bequeathed to the United States by James Smithson. The Institution is as an independent trust instrumentality of the United States holding more than 140 million artifacts and specimens in its trust for 'the increase and diffusion of knowledge.' The Institution is also a center for research dedicated to public education, national service, and scholarship in the arts, sciences, and history…. The Smithsonian is composed of sixteen museums and galleries and the National Zoo and numerous research facilities in the United States and abroad. Nine Smithsonian museums are located on the National Mall between the Washington Monument and the Capitol. Five other museums and the Zoo are elsewhere in Washington, D.C., and both the Cooper-Hewitt, National Design Museum and the National Museum of the American Indian Heye Center are in New York City." The building was completed in 1855, following the guidelines established for the Board of Regents: to build a "suitable building of plain and durable materials and structure, without unnecessary ornament, and of a sufficient size, and with suitable rooms or halls, for the reception and arrangement, upon a liberal scale of objects…." Far from plain but definitely durable, the old building is known as the "Castle" and is the center for Smithsonian operations.
Photography by James Blank

A summer concert by the United States Marine Band on the steps of the West Front of the Capitol

The Marine Band is known as "The President's Own," a title bestowed upon the group by President Thomas Jefferson during his inauguration in 1801 as the nation's third president. The band provides summer entertainment for citizens too.
Photography by Robert D. Shangle

The United States Botanic Garden

"The United States Botanic Garden traces its beginning to 1816, when the constitution of the Columbian Institute for the Promotion of Arts and Sciences in Washington, D.C., proposed the creation of a botanic garden to collect, grow, and distribute plants of this and other countries that might contribute to the welfare of the American people. The Institute's garden was established by Congress in 1820.... In 1842, the idea of a national botanic garden was re-established when the return of the United States Exploring Expedition to the South Seas (the Wilkes Expedition) brought to Washington a collection of living plants from around the globe.... The Garden [has been located at] its present location at First Street and Maryland Avenue, S.W. [since] 1933." *(www.aoc.gov/usbg/overview.htm)* A major remodeling effort began in 1997, (a five-year project) that includes the newly created National Garden. Featured in the Garden is the Environmental Learning Center, the Water Garden that honors the nation's First Ladies, and the new Rose Garden that features the National Flower; there is the Showcase Garden that displays an array of regional plants, the Butterfly Garden that features butterfly-attracting plants using color and aroma, and a Lawn Terrace for special events. The Botanic Garden is located on the National Mall across from the Capitol, and the National Garden is adjacent to the Conservatory.

Photography by James Blank

The White House from the South Lawn

Considered an "American Treasure," the White House is home to the President of the United States. It is also considered the "people's house." "President Jefferson … opened the house for public tours, and it has remained open, except during wartime, ever since. In addition, he welcomed visitors to annual receptions on New Year's Day and on the Fourth of July. In 1829, a horde of 20,000 Inaugural callers forced President Andrew Jackson to flee to the safety of a hotel while, on the lawn, aides filled washtubs with orange juice and whiskey to lure the mob out of the mud-tracked White House. … After Abraham Lincoln's presidency, Inaugural crowds became far too large for the White House to accommodate them comfortably. However, not until Grover Cleveland's first presidency did this unsafe practice change. He held a presidential review of the troops from a flag-draped grandstand built in front of the White House. This procession evolved into the official Inaugural parade we know today. Receptions on New Year's Day and the Fourth of July continued to be held until the early 1930s. … President Clinton's open house on January 21, 1993, renewed a venerable White House Inaugural tradition…."
Photography by James Blank

The Library of Congress

As the world's largest library, the nearly 119-million items are spread upon some 530 miles of bookshelves located in several locations. Three buildings comprise the mainstay of the Library. The familiar "Jefferson Building was opened to the public in 1897. The Library's design was based on the Paris Opera House and was unparalleled in national achievement. Its 23-carat gold-plated dome capped the 'largest, costliest, and safest' library building in the world. More than 40 painters and sculptors decorated the facade and interior making it surpass European libraries in its devotion to classical culture.… The building stands today as a unique blend of art and architecture and is recognized as a national treasure." The Adams Building opened in 1939 is capable of housing 10,000,000 volumes. And the James Madison Memorial Building completed in 1981 contains 2,100,000-square feet. Following the burning of the Capitol by the British during the War of 1812, where the Library was located, most of the books were destroyed. In 1815 Congress allocated funds for the purchase of Thomas Jefferson's personal library, which then gave the foundation to the Library of Congress, making "such books as may be necessary for the use of Congress" available. Millions of books, many extremely rare, recordings, photographs, maps, and manuscripts are housed within the confines of the Library of Congress, and thousands of new items are added daily.
Photography by Shangle Photographics

The United States Capitol and National Mall

"The National Mall's origins are as old as the capital city itself. The open space and parklands envisioned by Pierre L'Enfant's plan, which was commissioned by George Washington, created an ideal stage for national expressions of remembrance, observance and protest." *(www.nps.gov/nama/)*

Photography by Shangle Photographics

"Old Glory" at the Washington Monument

I pledge allegiance to the flag of the United States of America and to the Republic for which it stands, one Nation under God, indivisible, with liberty and justice for all. The Pledge was written by Francis Bellamy of Rome, New York, and published in "The Youth's Companion" on September 8, 1882. It was June 22, 1942 that Congress officially recognized the Pledge of Allegiance. Small word changes have occurred twice to the Pledge, on June 14, 1923 and June 14, 1954, National Flag Day in the United States.

Photography by Shangle Photographics

The Adams Building, opened in 1939, is capable of housing 10,000,000 volumes. And the James Madison Memorial Building completed in 1981 contains 2,100,000-square feet. All of this grew from the personal library of Thomas Jefferson, acquired by Congress in 1815, some 6,000 titles that replenished the book loss caused by the burning of the Capitol, a fire set by the British in 1814.

In a city of libraries the Library of Congress is breathtaking in its comprehensive nature. The reference service—established for the convenience of the United States Congress, but available to all—has no equal. Within the building the rococo marble staircase and the central reading room are indoor landmarks. The Library is not all books, even though it houses several hundred-thousand volumes of extremely rare titles including the Gutenberg Bible dating to around 1455. It is home to recordings, photographs, maps, and manuscripts, all increasing on a daily basis. The Coolidge Auditorium, located within the Jefferson Building presents some of the best musical interpretations in town.

No person of literary interest should leave the Hill without taking in the Folger Shakespeare Library, founded by Henry Clay Folger. The library was dedicated in 1932, two years following Folger's death. He and his wife, Emily Jordan Folger, who devoted efforts to see that the Library was completed, were ardent admirers of Shakespeare's works and endeavored to share their admiration with the people of the United States through their presentation of the Folger Shakespeare Library. Although Amherst College administers the library, benefactor Henry Clay Folger wisely directed that it be built in the highly accessible national capital. In addition to housing one of the world's greatest collection of English and Shakespeare literature, the Folger Library has a functional replica of an early 17th-century London theater and exhibits of Elizabethan life and customs.

As the visitor descends from Capitol Hill to The National Mall, the first attraction encountered is the U.S. Grant Memorial located on the grounds of the Botanic Garden. Sculptor Henry Merwin Shrady and architect, Edward Pearce Casey entered a contest in 1902 and won with their design, illustrating honor to the Union General. Among the District's statuary, the Grant Memorial is the biggest, mounted on a marble platform that extends 265 feet long; horse and rider rise to a height of 65 feet. The sculpture displays the attending tribute to Commanding General, Ulysses S. Grant. (Grant served his nation as the 18th President). One of the best of the many equestrian statues that decorate Washington's traffic circles honors the fighting Union General, Phil Sheridan, designed and created by Gutzon Borglum. Among the most moving (and non-equestrian) is Felix de Weldon's Marine Corps War Memorial in nearby Arlington, Virginia, just west of Washington, D. C., a section immediately identified with the capital city. (There are many locations found in Virginia and Maryland that are closely allied with the daily functions of the nation's capital. With the necessity of building expansion for the needs of the nation's business, federal development spread its boundaries to the nearby locations, maintaining the identity of Washington, D. C. power to broader sites).

Dominating the east end of The National Mall is the white marble expanse of the National Gallery of Art, flanked by a triumphantly modern East Wing. First known as the Mellon Gallery after its first benefactor, Andrew Mellon, the National Gallery has grown into one of the world's most important art museums. Traditionally, its immense collection has run toward old masters and European art. This policy is rapidly changing, especially with the advent of the East Wing, which features some spectacular contemporary outdoor sculpture. The National Gallery of Art states that it "houses one of the finest collections in the world illustrating major achievements in painting, sculpture, and graphic arts from the Middle Ages to the Present."

Before he does anything else, any American leaving the National

Gallery by the front entrance should dash across Constitution Avenue to the National Archives. There, after passing through the world's largest bronze doors, he can see with his own eyes three of history's most important documents, the Declaration of Independence, the United States Constitution, and the Bill of Rights. Elsewhere in the building, there are enough documents, microfilm, and curios to satisfy two hundred years of snooping. But these three original documents are the most significant in importance.

It is difficult to define the Smithsonian Institution. Known affectionately as "the Nation's attic," it is part museum, part archive, part art gallery, part publishing house, part science lab, part zoo, part theater, part concert hall, and much more. The Smithsonian has varying degrees of administrative responsibility for such diverse public charges as the National Gallery of Art, the National Zoo, the Smithsonian Tropical Research Area, the National Museum of Natural History, the National Postal Museum, and several more, totaling sixteen museums and galleries, nine of which are located along the National Mall. Crowning the paradox, it is a private foundation, charged by the government with these many tasks and given appropriations as necessary. Founder James Smithson bequeathed funds to found a society for the "increase of knowledge" in a country he never visited. If Smithson sought immortality, he achieved his goal, as the Smithsonian Institution is one of the more heavily visited sites in the United States. In 1904 the Englishman's body was brought to the United States for reburial in downtown Washington, D. C. The red-stone headquarters building, referred to as "the Castle," the Natural History Museum, the National and Technology Museum, and the National Air and Space Museum are the heart and soul of the Smithsonian Institution and The National Mall.

Aesthetically, the Washington Monument may be the most satisfying structure in the capital city. There is a kind of magic in the way its clean, vertical lines hover over a markedly horizontal city. At a height of 555 feet, 5 and 1/8th inches, the most visible landmark in the capital area, the Washington Monument is the tallest masonry structure in the world. It has nothing to fear locally from skyscrapers, because the Fine Arts Commission limits the height of a building in downtown Washington, D. C. At one time a favorite visitor's ritual was to climb the 989 steps to the top, but this is no longer permitted. Today, everyone must take the elevator and content himself with the challenge of reading 189 dedicatory inscriptions as they walk down the steps, if so inclined.

From the Washington Monument the obvious place to visit next is the Lincoln Memorial, located at the opposite end of the Reflecting Pool west of the Washington Monument. The building is remarkably compact for its size and its balance of horizontal and vertical lines complement perfectly the powerful upward thrust of the Monument and the rounded, rambling character of the Capitol, two miles east. The addition of the Reflecting Pool proved to be a stroke of genius. There is no question, either, about the impact of its interior. The chamber containing Daniel Chester French's giant statue of a brooding Abraham Lincoln has become one of the unofficial sanctuaries of the nation.

When the Kennedy Center for the Performing Arts opened in 1971, its opera house, concert hall, and theater instantly added a new dimension to cultural life in the capital. The world's leading artists vie to play the Kennedy Center. The Center is the vision of the distinguished American architect Edward Durell Stone. It has become one of the more popular meeting places of Washington's society.

With thousands of visitors each day lined up hoping to get in, the White House must be the best known residence in the country. It became white after British incendiaries scorched the sandstone exterior in 1914. Congress decided it would be cheaper to paint the president's house than to make repairs. It was not until the administration of Theodore Roosevelt, almost a century later, that the new title appeared on official presidential stationery. More than the most familiar residence, the White House may be the most renovated in the country. Each President has the prerogative of decorating the house as he sees fit. In Truman's administration, all but the third floor was completely renovated; the entire interior of the remaining building was scooped out and reconstructed, perhaps the most prodigious residential remodeling job ever undertaken. The history and decor of the East Room, the Blue Room, the Oval Office, the State Dining Room, and the Lincoln Bedroom are a familiar part of the national lore.

Historic Lafayette Square, named to honor General Marquis Gilbert de Lafayette of France, is located north of the White House across Pennsylvania Avenue. It was L'Enfant's intention that the area be the President's front yard and personal park. In proper fashion, George Washington did not approve of so much real estate being assigned to the Chief Executive and ordered the Square to be made into a public park. President Thomas Jefferson had Pennsylvania Avenue built in 1804 right through the park. The park, known as the President's Park, has been listed as a National Historic Landmark since 1970 and has been a National Park since August, 1933. Area surrounding the White House is included in the Park. Through much of the city's history, the Square was its most fashionable address. Today, the Square is largely institutionalized and only the Decatur House and the Dolly Madison House remain to represent the many historic mansions that once lined the park. St. John's Episcopal Church, "the church of the Presidents," actually faces 16th Street, but it is counted in the ambience of the Square. No one is quite sure why Andrew Jackson's statue holds the center of a park named for Lafayette, while the Marquis' statue is thrust into the southeast corner. It is best seen in late spring, when the magnolias are in bloom.

For those who appreciate fine architecture, do not miss the Old Executive Office Building just west of the White House. Built during Ulysses S. Grant's administration to house the Departments of State,

War, and Navy, it is a masterpiece of French Second Empire design, featuring columns upon columns, dormers, chimneys, and assorted decorated gimcracks to delight the eye. Inside the massive structure is a labyrinth of tiled hallways, lined in dark wood, which lead to an abundance of high ceilings, dark and comfortable appearing offices. Directly across Pennsylvania Avenue from "Old State" is the Blair House, the nation's official guest house. Understandably, neither building is open to the public.

The Work-a-day Capital

On any Monday morning, while the sightseer is still yawning in his hotel room, federal workers, civilian and military, are headed for their offices. They leave from red-brick row houses around Lincoln Park, estates in Potomac, garden apartments in Arlington, "dormitories" near DuPont Circle, stucco cottages in Takoma Park, ramblers in Silver Spring, and high-rise apartments in Rosslyn. By the tens of thousands, they stream into the Federal Triangle, the venerable, many winged Interior Department, the Department of Labor fortress near the Capitol, Foggy Bottom's State Department headquarters, the beautifully housed Department of Housing and Urban Development in L'Enfant Plaza, and many more.

Additional thousands travel away from the city toward the out of town sites favored by low profile officialdom: to the stolid whiteness of CIA headquarters in Langley, Virginia; the glassy expanse of the National Security Agency operations building at Fort Meade, Maryland; or the Department of Energy at Germantown, Maryland. The servants of the Republic travel mostly by private car, bus, and the sleek Metrorail system, which links points as distant as Laurel, Maryland,

and Dulles International Airport. By the time the visitor is ready to tackle the curving exhibit halls of the Hirshhorn Museum and Sculpture Garden, Uncle Sam's business is in high gear. Under the direction of the Smithsonian Institution, the museum states that "the Hirshhorn has one of the most comprehensive collections of modern sculpture in the United States or abroad. The collection's other strengths include contemporary art, European painting since World War II and American painting since the late 19th century.... The collection contains approximately 12,000 works of art, including some 5,000 paintings, 3,000 sculptures and mixed-media pieces, and 4,000 works on paper. About 600 works are on view in the galleries, plaza and garden at any one time."

The legendary Pentagon Building, the Defense Departments headquarters in Arlington, is hardly typical of federal work space. This is all the more reason for taking a closer look. The automobile parking covers sixty-seven acres of space for 8,770 vehicles, or sixteen separate parking lots. The Defense Department claims to have approximately 23,000 employees reporting to work in the five-sided building. The Pentagon was begun September, 1941, four months prior to the attack on Pearl Harbor, Hawaii, on December 7, 1941, and it was dedicated on January 15, 1943. The total cost of the building and outside facilities totaled an approximate $83,000,000. However, when all was said-and-done, the contents of seventeen buildings were placed within the walls of the new Defense Department headquarters. Depending upon whether the World Trade Center in New York is viewed as one building or a complex, the Pentagon may *still* be the world's largest office building. With its 6,636,360-square-feet of floor space, there can be no doubt that it is the world's largest five-story office building.

Even today the Pentagon's figures are still startling. There are 17.5 mile of corridors within the building that provide its occupants access to 691 drinking fountains, 284 rest rooms, 7,754 windows, 7,000 electric clock outlets, one dining room, two cafeterias, and six snack bars. The famous Concourse with its business services and miscellaneous shops might do service as a shopping mall in a small town. The building has 131 stairways, nineteen escalators, and thirteen elevators. Each section of its outer ring is 921 feet long. A lunchtime jog around the building would cover just about a mile's distance.

Architect G. E. Bergstrom's unusual design has proved to be functional and durable, and a bit mysterious as well. The five-story building has five concentric five-sided rings, connected by ten radial corridors and surrounding a central court that measures exactly five acres. All of this has raised speculation about its symbolism—the wagon train in a circle, for instance—but no one has come up with a totally convincing interpretation. In figurative language, the case has been quite different. Since the business of its tenants is of some concern to people of the world who speak a hundred or so different languages, "pentagon" may be the world's most widely and immediately understood metaphor. The building's non-dramatic configuration has worn well with most observers over the years, and it may be that the Pentagon, along with the Washington Monument, will survive changes in taste better than most other structures in Washington.

The frequent references to Washington, D. C. is "a one-industry city" or a "company town" can mislead the visitor about the true nature of the population. There is no denying that having 500,000-plus residents on a single payroll can create a tilt in the local economy. The real surprise in this figure is that it represents only about one-fourth of the capital area's work force. Contrary to popular notion, not everyone in Washington works for the Federal Government, not even indirectly. It stands to reason that government workers need to be housed, clothed, fed, transported, made secure, lobbied, entertained, spied on, and cured of affliction, both physical and spiritual. This calls for an abundant number of non-Federal help. We may speculate, then, that for each government stenographer, there is a hairdresser, a bank clerk, and a cocktail waitress; for each official in a regulatory agency, there are three lawyers in private practice. There is well over a million other wage earners in the metropolitan area whose work brings them only infrequently into direct contact with the activities of government.

In a curious way, a bit in the spirit of a medieval city, some of Washington, D. C.'s major streets attract to themselves particular activities. Massachusetts Avenue has long been "embassy row." Pennsylvania Avenue has always been very much a Federal boulevard, route of Presidents and Victorian armies. Connecticut Avenue is a business street—banks, offices, hotels, restaurants—in the spirit of the U. S. Chamber of Commerce, which stands at its foot. Sixteenth Street is the avenue of the national associations and, secondarily, an embassy row. Whatever L'Enfant's wishes were in the matter, the original naming of streets did not foresee a great growth. Numbering the north-south streets is an old American custom, handy because you can't conveniently run out of numbers, but lettering the east-west streets was another matter. Just as soon as the city had grown north by twenty-six blocks, there was a problem. This was resolved for the moment by beginning a new alphabet group of two-syllable names: Adams, Belmont, Chapin, etc. Progress pushed the city engineers through Upshur, Varnum, and Webster faster than anticipated. Postal letter carriers found themselves working a third alphabet group of three-syllable names: Allison, Buchanan, Crittenden. A fourth alphabet was inevitable. This group took horticultural names and mercifully the District boundary line ended the emergency at Verbena Street.

Through its first one-hundred years, Washington, D. C. scarcely rated a foreign embassy and not many delegations either. That is because it was not considered a very important capital. All of that attitude has changed. At a recent count, there were 176 embassies, most of them clustered along Massachusetts Avenue, N. W. between Dupont Circle and the Naval Observatory, home to the Vice President of the United States. It is not clear why Massachusetts Avenue attracted so many foreign missions, but it must have something to do with the availability of mansions and townhouses suitable to be converted to chancelleries. The large and attractive British Embassy, just below the Naval Observatory, has long ranked as one of the showcases of embassy row. The clean design of the Venezuelan Embassy on 30th Street also draws favorable comments.

Washington has on occasion been described as a city of churches. Since there are about five hundred churches in the area, this must refer to their architectural splendor. Washington Cathedral, the biggest of the churches in the District, dominates the skyline of northwest Washington, D. C., partly because of its size, and partly because it is on one of the highest spots in the city. The Cathedral is stated to be the sixth largest cathedral in the world and the second largest in the United States. Records indicate that President Theodore Roosevelt was present when the Cathedral's cornerstone was laid in 1907, and President George Herbert Walker Bush spoke when the final stone was set on September 29, 1990. The Basilica of the National Shrine of the Immaculate Conception, near Catholic University, looms above the thick trees in the residential northern half of the city. It is the largest Catholic Church in the Western Hemisphere and the eighth largest in the world. The two cathedrals offer a nice balance to the skyline of public buildings in downtown Washington. The Washington Cathedral is nominally Episcopalian, but it is open for use by all worshippers. In design it is the traditional Gothic, but there has been an effort in recent years to incorporate into the ambience the work of modern artists and artisans. It fits attractively into the popular Cathedral Close, one of Washington's favorite gardens. It has the admirable feature of being all masonry. For many of the visitors to Washington, D. C., their visit would not be complete without viewing the white marbled Washington Temple and Visitor Center. Prior to the Temple dedication in 1974, a reported 758,000 people visited the beautiful structure. The Mormon Temple grounds are spread over fifty-seven acres of beautifully landscaped grounds bedecked with floral gardens. The

Visitor Center welcomes all people, while the Temple is only open to members of the church.

Among the most interesting and attractive ecclesiastical buildings in the city is the Washington Mosque on Massachusetts Avenue above Sheridan Circle. The limestone shrine is the center of Islamic worship in Washington, D. C. and is shared by members of the many foreign missions from Moslem nations.

Georgetown

Georgetown may be America's most fashionable address. Actually, the United States Postal Service won't let you use Georgetown as the address for delivery purposes, at least not since 1895 when the town officially became part of Washington, D. C. However, if you cannot have Georgetown *for an address,* you can still manage a Georgetown address. Of course you may have to content yourself with a prosaic legend like 2715 Q Street, N. W., Washington, D. C., 20007. But this should not cause worry. Any Washington hostess who knows her P and Q streets will recognize instantly that it falls within the enchanted enclave. Prosaic or not, anyone should be more than content with that address. It is that of the elegant Dumbarton House, maintained as an historic shrine.

Georgetown was first settled in the 17th century as a thriving river port town and was chartered by the Crown, all before Pierre L'Enfant was even born. To the chagrin of a few socially sensitive Georgetowners, however, it was discovered not long ago that the town was not named for one of the Hanoverian kings but for a Scottish indentured servant who was the area's first squatter. George Washington, who lived less than fifteen miles down river from the settlement, frequented the little town throughout his life. It was at Suter's Tavern, somewhere near present day K Street, N. W., that he called the first meeting of commissioners to discuss plans for the new federal capital.

"If Georgetown is just a part of Washington, D. C. now," asks the visitor, "how can I tell when I'm there?" Well, if you find yourself walking for a succession of blocks over quaint but sometimes uneven brick sidewalks; through quiet streets where elms sometimes arch the roadway; past dozens and dozens of handsome federal-style Victorian and modern townhouses, most sporting polished brass door knockers, you are probably in Georgetown. If you are on a teeming commercial street, it suddenly strikes you that art galleries outnumber the fast food restaurants, you know for sure that you are in Georgetown. If you are one who craves a more concrete orientation, know that as you cross Rock Creek Parkway traveling west on M Street, N. W. you are in Georgetown the instant the front bumper of your car reaches the intersection with Pennsylvania Avenue. After all the articles and descriptive matter that appears in the guide books about stately Georgetown, the visitor might be disconcerted by the strong commercial character of M Street. He will discover to his relief that almost all business in Georgetown is confined to this street and to Wisconsin Avenue.

Right in the midst of the crush of boutiques, restaurants, and nightclubs is one of the oldest surviving structures in the Washington area, the Old Stone House built in 1765. This 18th-century house was home to an average colonial family of the day, and it offers a view of middle class life of the period. It is maintained by the National Park Service and is available to the public as a museum. At the east end of the same block is a fine old 18th-century structure, the Thomas Sim Lee Corner, the first Georgetown building saved from the wrecker's ball under the provision of the Old Georgetown Act.

Congress passed the Old Georgetown Act with the expressed intent to help preserve historically or architecturally important buildings within Georgetown. It also restored a measure of the former town's identity. For example Georgetowners were permitted to raise street signs that added old street names—Needwood, Wapping, Gay, East Lane, Cherry Alley, *et al.*—to those imposed by the Postal Service. The story of Francis Scott Key Bridge, which links Georgetown to Arlington, Virginia, is a parable illustrating why the Old Georgetown Act is necessary. In the 1920s Congress authorized construction of the graceful span to succeed the old Aqueduct Bridge and honor the memory of Georgetown's most famous native son. The building contractors promptly tore down the house that Francis Scott Key had been born in to make way for the approaches to the new bridge.

From M Street the visitor is well advised to divert a block south to see the old Chesapeake & Ohio (C&O) Canal before tackling the main part of Georgetown. The historic canal, which floated its last payload in 1924, runs the length of Georgetown parallel to the K Street Viaduct and continues all the way to Cumberland, Maryland. Large stretches of the canal are maintained by the National Park Service, being acquired September 23, 1928, and becoming a National Historical Park on January 8, 1971. George Washington was one of the early boosters and stockholders in the Canal Company, but it didn't open until 1828. The appearance of railroad service reduced its initial importance. As a tourist attraction, the old canal has probably returned its construction cost several times over. The canal towpath is one of the capital's most popular hiking routes. In the Georgetown section, the tiny colorful houses that line the canal—called with disarming logic the Towpath Houses—are a choice location for many of Washington's residents.

Georgetown has between forty and fifty houses of historic distinction and not all of them are row houses or townhouses. A few are mansions on small estates. Tudor Place on 31st Street is one of the larger dwellings, and by consensus one of Georgetown's most attractive. "Tudor" is a misnomer: the house is a distinguished representative of Federal-design stucco exterior. It was created by Dr. William Thornton, designer of the Capitol, and completed in 1816 by Thomas Peters and his wife Martha Parke Custis, a granddaughter of Martha Dandridge Custis Washington, wife of George Washington. The house was continuously occupied by the Custis-Peters family until 1984, a total of six generations. As a public museum, a tour includes viewing family heirlooms, furnishings, manuscripts, and photographs that provide an insight to the family's legacy.

Even Washingtonians sometimes get confused about the difference between Dumbarton House and Dumbarton Oaks. Dumbarton House is the genteel late-Georgian house on Q Street, and it could claim to be the oldest house in Georgetown. Dumbarton Oaks is a small urban estate lying north of R Street and west of Oak Hill Cemetery. It may lie outside the boundaries established by the Old Georgetown Act, but no matter. It fits in beautifully with everything else. The 19th-century mansion is now a museum of Byzantine and Roman art and is administered by Harvard University. Mildred and Robert Woods Bliss bequeathed sixteen acres of the fifty-three acre estate that included the house, gardens, and their collections to the University in 1940 to establish the Dumbarton Oaks Research Library and Collection. Robert Woods Bliss was a retiring man who was born in St. Louis, Missouri, on August 5, 1875. He served his country as a Foreign Service officer, Minister to Sweden, and the U. S. Ambassador to Argentina. After World War II, Dumbarton Oaks was used as the meeting location that led to the formation of the United Nations. Mr. Bliss died in Washington, D. C. on April 19, 1962.

Georgetown has the singular good fortune to be bound by belts of green on almost every side: on the east by Rock Creek Parkway; on the west by the largest swatch of ground, the campus of Georgetown University. Founded by the first head of the American Catholic Church in the late 1780s, Bishop John Carroll located sixty acres of ground and opened Georgetown University in January, 1792, overlooking the village of Georgetown. The school received its first charter from the United States government in 1815.

Georgetown can be both a joy and a frustration to the visitor. While its charming streets may have the air of a museum, or may even conjure up recollections of historic restorations like Williamsburg and Sturbridge Village, the fact is that entire families have regular daily lives where they work and play behind almost every one of those polished door knockers. Unless you happen to know a resident or two, there is no way you can discover what those glamorous houses look like inside. There is one exception. Sometime in the spring a number of Georgetowner's open their houses and gardens for annual tours. If you are lucky, enterprising, or downright aggressive, you might obtain a ticket to one of those tours. Gardens, incidentally, are another thing secluded behind most of the handsome facades, an estimated 4,000 of them, some very tiny. The garden at Dumbarton Oaks, open to the public most of the year, is most likely the biggest by far.

The American Creed

"I believe in the United States of America as a government of the people, by the people, for the people; whose just powers are derived from the consent of the governed; a democracy in a republic; a sovereign Nation of many sovereign States; a perfect union, one and inseparable, established upon those principles of freedom, equality, justice and humanity for which American patriots sacrificed their lives and fortunes."

"I therefore believe it is my duty to my country to love it, to support its Constitution, to obey its laws, to respect its flag, and to defend it against all enemies."

William Tyler Page,
Clerk of the U. S. House of Representatives,
wrote "The American Creed" in 1917.
It was accepted by the House on behalf of the American
people on April 3, 1918.

The Green Hills

No major city in America is more fortunate than Washington, D. C. in the beauty, variety, and generally unspoiled character of its environs—near and far. It is a remarkable turn of events when one considers that this Upper Potomac River location was agreed upon not for reasons of its natural endowments, but on grounds of geography and then purely as a matter of political expediency. In 1790 Thomas Jefferson entertained Alexander Hamilton at a gentlemanly dinner in New York, and the two men came to a gentleman's agreement. Jefferson would support Hamilton's important money bill in Congress (regarding one standard currency for the nation and the establishment of the First Bank of the United States), and Hamilton would use his influence to locate the new federal capital outside the teeming Northeast section of the new country. The compromise pointed inevitably to a site on the Potomac River, which lay just about halfway between Boston, Massachusetts, and Charleston, South Carolina.

Washington, D. C. lies midway between the Appalachian foothills on the west and the Chesapeake Bay wetlands on the east. In this part of the country, there can be a remarkable variation in terrain, even within a short distance. Although downtown Washington is flat and marshy, the terrain rises rapidly in all directions, from about sea level at the Zero Milestone on the Ellipse to over 400 feet at the beginning of the third alphabet on Connecticut Avenue, less than four miles away. Except to the northeast, where the land gradually flattens into the sandy, piney estuary country, the countryside around the capital is one of low, rolling hills, noticeably free of the landmarks of heavy industry that have become the heritage of so many cities.

One of the best spots from which to gain an appreciation of Washington's favored situation is less than a mile from the Lincoln Memorial, the Arlington National Cemetery, located across the Potomac River in Virginia. Two of the most moving prospects at Arlington is from the porch of the Custis-Lee Mansion, now officially called the Arlington House, and the Tomb of the Unknown Soldier. Looking across the river east toward the capital from even this short distance affords an impression of a clean and spacious city encircled by pleasant green hills. Arlington National Cemetery, in fact, may be the very best place for any visitor to begin a look around at Washington, D. C.'s environs. As the most famous American military cemetery, Arlington contains the graves of many national heroes as well as the graves of over 250,000 veterans of the Armed Forces, totaling over 260,000 people. The two most often visited gravesites in the park are those of the Unknown Soldier and the assassinated President John F. Kennedy. Veterans as diverse in fame as Earl Warren, William Jennings Bryan, Phil Sheridan, Pierre L'Enfant, and John Foster Dulles are also buried at Arlington National Cemetery.

The presence of the attractive Custis-Lee Mansion in the cemetery is anomalous and a reminder that it became a military cemetery by chance. Once the home of General Robert E. Lee, commander of the Confederate army, the mansion was seized by the Union Army to be used as a headquarters building. With the arrival of so many dead soldiers from the many battles in nearby northern Virginia, the Army began to bury the bodies on the slopes below the mansion. After the war Lee never got his property back. Following the death of General Lee in 1870, the eldest son of General and Mrs. Lee, Custis Lee, realized the return of the property in 1882 after filing a lawsuit for illegal confiscation. The Federal Government purchased the property from Custis Lee on March 3, 1883, for $150,000. And so the advent of a national cemetery.

No one should leave Arlington without seeing the Marine Corps War Memorial, the Iwo Jima Monument in the northern corner just off Arlington Boulevard. Sculptor Felix de Weldon's massive bronze group was modeled after Joe Rosenthal's famous news photo taken atop Mount Suribachi on Iwo Jima, Japan. It is usually identified instantly by young and old alike. It is one of the largest statues in the capital and it is appropriately placed close to one of the area's busiest roadways.

Fifteen miles down river from Arlington is Mount Vernon, the comely estate of a man who knew well and deeply appreciated the charms of the local countryside. No matter the cost in time and money, every American should make the pilgrimage to the restored home of George Washington. The place speaks volumes about the kind of men who made the American Revolution. No romantic, intellectual revolutionaries here. The master of Mount Vernon and his colleagues from north and south alike were prosperous men, energetic men, and optimistic men. In the Age of Reason, they never hesitated to apply it, but they applied it largely to getting things done, and with luck, turning a profit. Listen to the tour guide tell about Mount Vernon's 8,000 acres of tobacco, cereal grains, and other crops. Listen and learn about the hundreds of head of livestock that grazed the fields; about the garden, the craft shops, and the hundreds of workers, most of whom had to be fed right on the plantation. Handling the Presidency must have seemed easier by comparison. About 150 years before Calvin Coolidge, in his Vermont candor, articulated the national creed when sworn in as the nation's thirtieth president, George Washington must have understood that "the business of America is business."

Those who drive down the George Washington Memorial Parkway to Mount Vernon can take comfort in their great flexibility of schedule. There is time to visit Alexandria, Virginia's charming Old Town. There is an opportunity to stop off at the George Washington Masonic National Memorial, in design, one of the most curious buildings in the capital area. The view of Washington, D. C. from the Memorial may be even better than the view from Arlington House.

The Mount Vernon estate, now reduced to forty acres, has been preserved, restored, and is lovingly maintained by the Mount Vernon Ladies Association. In the 1850s over much hard headed 19th-century resistance, the Association saved the estate from being turned into a hotel and probably eventually demolished. Not a nickel of tax payer's money went into its salvation. The ladies raised all of the money from private donors. To get the proper feel of the place, the visitor should allow not less than half-a-day for wandering, snooping, and reflecting. Even at its present forty acres, it is extremely impressive with its tree lined avenues, extensive formal gardens, its dozen or more original outbuildings, the well manicured grounds and, of course, the mansion house itself. Away from the house is the tomb of George and Martha Washington. Despite the greater durability (and dampness) of their stone manor houses, few Englishmen of Washington's day could have lived in more baronial splendor than as Washington did in his fashionable home.

On the Maryland side of the Potomac River, the most attractive route into the backcountry is by consensus the C & O Canal Towpath. Hiking along the towpath may come close to being the single most popular outdoor activity among Washingtonians. The picturesque path, beautifully graded by the pounding of mule hoofs over the century of time, is now part of a Historic National Park that extends from the Canal's tidewater terminus in Georgetown to Cumberland,

Maryland, 185 miles away in the mountains of western Maryland. It is possible to hike the full distance, taking advantage of Park Service campsites along the way. Most Washingtonians content themselves with the stretch between Georgetown and Seneca, Maryland. Some of the locks and the old lock houses have been restored and help to add color to the Canal scene.

Perhaps the outstanding scenic attraction along the Canal's route can be found just seven miles upstream from the District of Columbia boundary line—the Great Falls of the Potomac. Here the river comes crashing through a rocky gorge about a mile long, dropping more than seventy five feet. It is difficult to believe that this is the same river that one sees at Memorial Bridge in Washington, and clearly it is one of the things that must have stimulated the building of the C & O Canal. There are two parks here, a state park on the Virginia side in addition to the National Historic Park. On the Maryland side, there are sturdy walkways built over jagged rocks and white water. Alongside the Canal at this point is Great Falls Tavern, built in 1839 and now converted to a museum and Park Service Information Center. The Tavern once offered accommodations to travelers using the canal boats. An average barge speed of two-miles-per-hour suggests that there once must have been more of these hostelries along the Canal's 185-mile length.

The attractive countryside around the capital was coveted early on for a type of suburban living associated with the raising and riding of horses. This was true on both the Virginia and Maryland sides of the Potomac River. There was a time not many years ago when one might see the "hunt country" estates not far from the center of Washington. However, the rapid increase in population in the metropolitan area and the consequent spread of urban density has consigned this bucolic idyll to areas well beyond the Capital Beltway. However, in places as far out as Middleburg and Warrenton, Virginia, one can still find the stately white mansions sitting on green hillocks and well seated squires cantering on quiet dirt pathways.

More representative of suburban living in the future is Reston, Virginia, about six miles east of Dulles International Airport. Reston was designed in the early 1960s as a self-contained small city, planned down to the last detail. It has both high and low density neighborhoods, big and small apartment buildings, townhouses, mansions, parks, churches, medical facilities, stores, theaters, even its own lake.

Any visitor who drives as far as Reston should go the extra few miles to Dulles International Airport to see the extraordinary terminal building. The giant but strikingly graceful structure looks as though it might achieve flight with greater ease than the aircraft sitting on its runways.

Another stop worth making in this area is at Wolf Trap Farm Park for the Performing Arts located right off the Dulles access road in Vienna, Virginia. Few of the musicians and other artists who appear here in summer can have performed elsewhere in such beautiful natural surroundings. Wolf Trap Farm is the only National Park in the United States dedicated to the Performing Arts. The Filene Center is the focal point of the Park, and the National Park Service states that it is "Wolf Trap's largest venue. It is an open-air performing arts pavilion that can accommodate an audience of 7,028. This include[s] 3,868 in-house seats (with an 88-seat orchestra pit) and 3,160 seats on its sloping lawn. This facility and several others are situated in a setting of rolling hills and woods located on 130 acres of National Park land. Through the unique partnership and collaboration of the National Park Service and the Wolf Trap Foundation, Wolf Trap Farm Park offers a wealth of both natural and cultural resources to the community and to the nation."

Points of Interest
Pictured in this book

Additional Points of Interest

African-American Civil War Museum
Albert Einstein Memorial
American University
Anacostia Museum
Anderson House
Andrews Air Force Base
Arlington House
Arthur M. Sackler Gallery
Blair House
C & O Canal
Capitol Childrens Museum
Christ Church, Arlington
Clara Barton National Historic Site
Constitution Gardens
Corcoran Gallery of Art
DAR Museum & Constitution Hall
Decatur House
Dumbarton House
Dumbarton Oaks
Explorers Hall, National Geographic Society
Folger Shakespeare Library
Fort Myer
Fransican Monastery
Frederick Douglass National Historic Site
Freer Gallery of Art
George Washington Masonic National Memorial
Georgetown
Goddard Space Flight Center
Great Falls Park
Gunston Hall Plantation
Hirshhorn Museum and Sculpture Garden
Historical Society of Washington, D. C.

Islamic Center
Kenilworth Aquatic Gardens
Kreeger Museum
L'Enfant Plaza
Martin Luther King, Jr., Library
Memorial to Signers of the Declaration of Independence
NASA-Goddard Visitors Center
National Aquarium
National Building Museum
National Capitol Trolley Museum
National Gallery of Art
National Law Enforcement Officers Memorial
National Library of Medicine
National Museum of African Art
National Museum of American Jewish Military History
National Museum of Health & Medicine
National Museum of Natural History
National Museum of Women in the Arts.
National Portrait Gallery
National Postal Museum
National Zoological Park
Navy Museum
Octagon
Old Presbyterian Meeting House
Old Stone House
Oxon Hill Farm
Pentagon
Renwick Gallery
Robert Taft Memorial
Rock Creek Cemetery
Sewall-Belmont House
St. Matthew's Cathedral
Textile Museum
Tudor Place
U. S. Chess Hall of Fame & Museum

U. S. Navy Memorial & Naval Heritage Center
United States Holocaust Memorial Museum
United States National Arboretum
Washington Dolls' House & Toy Museum
Woodrow Wilson House

National Park Areas

Anacostia Park
Battleground National Cemetery
Capitol Hill Parks
Chesapeake & Ohio Canal National Historical Park
Constitution Gardens
Ford's Theatre National Historic Site
For Dupont Park
Franklin Delano Roosevelt Memorial
Frederick Douglass National Historic Site
Kenilworth Park & Aquatic Gardens
Korean War Veterans Memorial
Lincoln Memorial
Mary McLeod Bethune Council House National Historic Site
National Capital Parks-Central
National Capital Parks-East
National Mall
Old Post Office Tower
Peirce Mill
Pennsylvania Avenue National Historic Site
Potomac Heritage National Scenic Trail
President's Park (White House)
Rock Creek Park
Sewall-Belmont House National Historic Site
The Old Stone House
Thomas Jefferson Memorial
Vietnam Veterans Memorial
Washington Monument

About the Constitution of the United States of America

The governing power of the United States of America is embodied by the Constitution, adopted September 17, 1787. As simple as this may sound, it is far from a quickly composed instrument. Its strength encompasses efforts of powerful, intellectual minds who endeavored to create a written instrument that provides self government, independence of mind and thought, and the right of man to move forward in a free, unencumbered way of life. Based on the ideal of Federalism (preferring a centralized national government), the authors of the United States Constitution protected against "power by few" by dividing authority into three branches of government: the executive, the judicial, and the legislative. Employing the "checks and balances" system, each branch monitors the activities of the other two branches, striving to keep a balance among the three.

With the knowledge acquired from previous governmental instruments and from the actions of the people, the Constitutional framers understood the ramifications of the written word. The Magna Carta, adopted by the British Monarchy and ruling Barons in 1215, provided for the beginning of protection of civil liberties. In 1620 the "Separationists," more commonly identified today as the Pilgrims, joined together on the ship *Mayflower* and sailed to the New World, seeking freedom from religious persecution. Upon their arrival and before disembarking the ship, the Pilgrims composed an instrument known as The Mayflower Compact designed for self government that would allow the banding together "to enact, constitute and frame such just and equal Laws, Ordinances, Acts, Constitutions and Offices" needed for the convenience of governing.

As immigrants established homes, created businesses, churches, and a way of life in the New World, the desire for self preservation was strong. As generations of people sprang forth; ties to the Mother Country began to fade for many. The independent strength of the New World citizen sent out deep roots that developed societal structure and established new heritage conviction. Many felt the need for "independence" from British rule, providing the impetus for the American Revolution.

In June of 1776 Thomas Jefferson was appointed by the Continental Congress to draft a resolution with the expressed intent of declaring the Colonies "free and independent states ... absolved from allegiance to the British Crown." On July 2, 1776, after many hours and over many days of revision by Jefferson and members of Congress, the Declaration of Independence was completed, and on July 4, 1776, the Declaration was adopted by Congress.

In January, 1777, Congress began the chore of composing The Articles of Confederation, a document used for the purpose of unification of rule by the original thirteen colonies, while maintaining state freedom and independence for its citizens. The voluminous document containing thirteen articles was finally adopted November 15, 1777. Not taken lightly by any of the Colonies, it was a four-year process before all thirteen Colonies ratified the Articles of Confederation, becoming into force March 1, 1781.

Following the victory by the Patriots over the British, Congress realized the inadequacy of the Articles of Confederation and the need for a stronger federal union. On February 12, 1787, the monumental task of revising the Articles was undertaken. A three-branch governmental plan was created: Executive (Presidential, Judicial (Supreme Court), and Legislative (Congress). The Legislative allowed for two chambers of control: the Senate or Upper House having two members per state with one vote each; the House of Representatives or Lower House having its members determined by the populace census of each state. Seven months later, on September 17, 1787, the Constitution of the United States was signed and established by Congress.

The strength of the Constitution has been tested over the many years, accepting challenges by such confrontations as the Civil War, a grueling threat to the Federal Union. By its flexibility and inherent wisdom, the Constitution has provided the foundation of guidance to govern the citizens of the United States of America for over 200 years.

Preamble to the Constitution

We the People of the United States,
In Order to form a more perfect Union,
establish Justice,
insure domestic Tranquility,
provide for the common Defence,
promote the general Welfare,
and secure the Blessings of Liberty to
ourselves and our Posterity,
do ordain and establish the Constitution
for the United States of America.